T0094511

50 American
Plays
(Poems)

Also by Matthew Dickman

All-American Poem

Also by Michael Dickman

The End of the West
Flies

Matthew Dickman & Michael Dickman

50 American Plays

(Poems)

COPPER CANYON PRESS

PORT TOWNSEND, WASHINGTON

Copper Canyon Press is in residence at Fort Worden State Park in Port Townsend, Washington, under the auspices of Centrum. Centrum is a gathering place for artists and creative thinkers from around the world, students of all ages and backgrounds, and audiences seeking extraordinary cultural enrichment.

LIBRARY OF CONGRESS CATALOGING-IN-PUBLICATION DATA
Dickman, Matthew.
  50 American plays : poems / Matthew Dickman and Michael Dickman.
    p. cm.
  ISBN 978-1-55659-393-2 (ALK. PAPER)
  I. Dickman, Michael, 1975- II. Title. III. Title: Fifty American plays.

PS3604.I2988A615 2012
811'.6—DC23

                        2011044747

98765432 first printing

COPPER CANYON PRESS
Post Office Box 271
Port Townsend, Washington 98368
www.coppercanyonpress.org

"These States!" as Whitman said, whatever he meant.

—D.H. Lawrence, "The Evening Land"

In all plays, even *Hamlet*, the scenery is the best part.

—John Ashbery, "Cliffhanger"

50 American Plays
(Poems)

Duke Ellington Addresses the Fields of Alabama

ELLINGTON.

     Come Sunday

     The light is going

     To really break you open

     Really break you apart

     Really move

     The blood out from the fields

     There is nothing

     No there is nothing

     Like cotton husks

     Like cotton hands

     To make them want

     To hear music

     Nothing! Nothing! Nothing!

     You broke

     Our backs

     A B-flat!

     A heartbreaking B-flat

     For the fields of Alabama

Love in Alaska

(*It's light out all night long*)

ALASKA.
        I want you to fuck me

BAKED ALASKA.
        I can't

ALASKA.
        I'm sorry you can't

BAKED ALASKA.
        You're always sorry

ALASKA.
        That's not what I mean, I mean—

BAKED ALASKA.
        Look, my body doesn't want to touch your body

ALASKA.
        Your body

BAKED ALASKA.
        No, it doesn't

(*It's still light out*)

People Retire to Arizona for Lots of Reasons

(*Sunsets and deserts*)

AN OLD MAN.
 Golf clubs

AN OLD WOMAN.
 Look like

AN OLD MAN.
 Long

AN OLD WOMAN.
 Silver

AN OLD MAN.
 Glittering

AN OLD WOMAN.
 Shining

AN OLD MAN.
 Spears

AN OLD WOMAN.
 Or arrows

AN OLD MAN.
 Or wings

AN OLD WOMAN.
 Of angels

AN OLD MAN.
 Coming

AN OLD WOMAN.
 To get us

AN OLD MAN.
 Different from Florida

The Moonlight in Arkansas Is Almost a Song

MOONLIGHT.

The way the trees

All down Main Street

Seem to drip

With silver acetone

How the newly new buildings

Cast themselves

Against the past—

That entire neighborhoods

Look like black-

And-white movies

A lot of the pain disappears into the backlit edges of
hedges

Some people

Are dancing beneath

Broken streetlights

You are

The Swimming Pools of California

(California light comes waltzing in across the swimming pool)

A YOUNG MAN.
> I'd like a little something to brighten up my drink

A YOUNG WOMAN.
> Maybe an ice cube would you like an ice cube?

A YOUNG MAN.
> That sounds great

A YOUNG WOMAN.
> And maybe a twist of lemon?

A YOUNG MAN.
> Yes a twist of lemon and a splash more vodka

A YOUNG WOMAN.
> A splash more vodka

A YOUNG MAN.
> You better make it a couple splashes

A YOUNG WOMAN.
> A couple three or four splashes and ice and a twist of lemon

A YOUNG MAN.
> A lemon from our very own lemon tree

A YOUNG WOMAN.
> We grow our lemons for just this very thing

Colorado Is a Sportsman's Paradise

(*Many Mountains*)

A HIKER.

> Could you move that a little to the left?

A MOUNTAIN.

> Things are happening

(*Fewer Mountains*)

The Trains in Connecticut Used to Run on Coal

(*A Man in blackface performs an elaborate tap dance down the aisle of a train, pouring coffee and shining shoes and carrying luggage and refusing tips*)

(*He stops*)

(*He still stops*)

(*He won't start again*)

CONNECTICUT PORTER.
AAAAAAAAAAAAAAAAAAAAAAAAAAAAAAAALL
ABOARD!

Let's Do It in Delaware

(*A hotel*)

DELEGATE 1.
>Do you think you could at least try?

DELEGATE 2.
>Yes, I'll try

DELEGATE 1.
>Okay, I'll lie down like this like I'm sleeping and you enter from the other room

DELEGATE 2.
>Good, then I'll climb on and pin you down

DELEGATE 1.
>Good, with your hands around my throat

DELEGATE 2.
>With or without the mask?

DELEGATE 1.
>With

DELEGATE 2.
>And then you're going to get it

DELEGATE 1.
>And then you're going to get it

(*A hotel humming*)

For Ernie Casciato

Acknowledgments

Grateful acknowledgment is due the editors of the following magazines where some of the *50 American Plays* first appeared: *Fence, Narrative, Poor Claudia.*

Thanks to Provincetown Theater for hosting a staged reading of an earlier version of *50 American Plays* in 2006.

Thanks also to our friends and family, especially our mother, Wendy Dickman: *first audience, first director.*

Walt Disney Doesn't Give a Shit About Florida

WALT.

       I want to say that it was a dream about orange groves and the light in the orange groves and the idea behind oranges of orange juice cold as blue tile against the bottom of your bare feet in the morning as oranges sat quietly in a quiet blue glass pitcher on the counter and how it was waiting for small children like a little sun floating in juice glasses and it would seem like a moment to them later of agelessness and they could be children forever even though it was a memory and we could all stay like children and our parents and grandparents could relax beneath the palm trees which was another part of the dream and I never dreamt of Cuban children on little rafts made of tires trying not to die in the ocean unless they were pirates which they were but that wasn't the dream it wasn't oranges and little kiddies running around I guess mostly I dreamt about money and mice

ORANGE GROVE WORKER.

       And?

WALT.

       And the singing Jews

ORANGE GROVE WORKER.

       And?

WALT.

       And the dancing Blacks

The Haiku Poets of Georgia

GEORGIA PEACH.
When I sway like this
I feel like a tall woman
The moon ass-grabbing

GEORGIA ON MY MIND.
I could dance all night
Everything smells like oceans
Night skins why is that?

SOUTHERN HOSPITALITY.
I love your new dress
I'LL FUCKING KILL YOU FUCKING!
I love your new dress

Kenneth Koch Directs *Hamlet* in Hawaii

KOCH.

> You don't see your father
>
> You
>
> *Feel* your father

Visit the Beautiful State Parks of Idaho

BEAR.

> In the old days we couldn't give away the blackberries

RANGER.

> Well, now there's more to consider, recreational tax cuts
> et cetera

BEAR.

> My spirit animal is going to eat your spirit animal

RANGER.

> I want you to!

(*The Bear's spirit animal eats the Ranger's spirit animal*)

BEAR.

> You were a good ranger
>
> Walking carefully
>
> Between the trees
>
> Putting out
>
> Fires

The Lost Indians of Illinois Return for One Last Song

(*Tents and small fires*)

CHIEF.

> The tents

SQUAW.

> And the small fires

HUNTER.

> Made space

GATHERER.

> In the mind

WARRIOR.

> For bigger fires

CHIEF.

> And the tents

SQUAW.

> In the mind

HUNTER.

> Opened

GATHERER.

> Their little flaps

WARRIOR.

> For the stars

CHIEF.

> Like the tips

SQUAW.

> Of arrows

HUNTER.

      The tips

GATHERER.

      The very tips

The Coldest Weather in Indiana

SNOW.

       Draped like lace

       Between the fencepost

       And the sky

       I spend all my time

       Thinking of

       Disappearing

       Thinking of water

       Of churches

       And drowning

       It's an idea

       For the world

       And not just

       The great Midwest

       A slow melt

       But you don't have to drown

       Draped like lace

       Between the frozen

       And dangerous

       Fenceposts!

Kenneth Koch Plays Ophelia to a Packed House in Iowa

(A child's swimming pool, Koch in drag)

KOCH.

You could drown

In your own vomit around here

And no one would notice

Be careful

Of standing behind curtains

And wine that has turned

And advice from adults

And advice from the dead

And sword fights

And Fortinbras

And Stepmothers

And stage directions

And nuns

And his skin

And his lips

And his eyes

And flowers

And flowers

And flowers

Lucky in Kansas

JUDY GARLAND.

This is always the worst part

TIN MAN.

The coming back

JUDY GARLAND.

It sucks, it sucks it's depressing as shit

THE LION.

Well we're lucky to still be employed at this farm

SCARECROW.

I wouldn't call it lucky

THE LION.

We were lucky to get back

SCARECROW.

That's not really lucky either I don't think you know
what lucky means

JUDY GARLAND.

It's funny what you miss

TIN MAN.

The running

JUDY GARLAND.

The flying

TIN MAN.

The flying monkeys

JUDY GARLAND.

The beautiful flying monkeys above the endless
emeralds the unbelievably green world

Punchy in Kentucky

(*A backyard. A bottle of beer. Two bottles*)

FATHER.

I want you to punch me

SON.

I don't want to punch you

FATHER.

Of course you do. Come on. I deserve it. Punch me

SON.

It's not—

FATHER.

Yes it will! You'll feel a lot better. Now hurry up before it gets dark

(*It gets dark*)

SON.

IDON'TWANTTOFUCKINGPUNCHYOU!

FATHER.

No

No, you don't

A Tailgate for the Southern Poets of Louisiana State University Press

CHEERLEADER.

T.R. Hummer?

T.R. HUMMER.

Yes!

CHEERLEADER.

Have a beer! Dave Smith?

DAVE SMITH.

Here!

CHEERLEADER.

Have a beer! James Applewhite?

JAMES APPLEWHITE.

Yes!

CHEERLEADER.

Have a beer! Margaret Gibson?

MARGARET GIBSON.

Here!

CHEERLEADER.

Have a beer! Marilyn Nelson?

MARILYN NELSON.

Yes!

CHEERLEADER.

Have a beer! Fred Chappell?

FRED CHAPPELL.

Here!

CHEERLEADER.

Have a beer!

FRED CHAPPELL.

I'll have two. And the moon! Two moons!

Maine Seafood Company

(*Salt*)

A LOBSTER.

    Once out of the box

    The wooden box The metal box

    The box, the box, the box!

    Dragged up from the salt

    Things don't feel too bad

    And then they do

    And then they don't

(*And waves*)

The Little-Known Japanese Internment Camps of Maryland

(*Fences, houses, laundry*)

JAPANESE MAN.
> The rice
>
> Goes bad
>
> No matter what

JAPANESE WOMAN.
> I almost miss the Chinese!

(*Cole Porter's hit tune "Don't Fence Me In"*)

The Past in Massachusetts

(*A long table, pumpkins*)

PILGRIM.

    Sometimes I think I could eat nothing but corn for the rest of my life

INDIAN.

    Thanks for the blankets

WITCHES.

    We can float! We can float! We can float!

VILLAGE PRIEST.

    If you like that

    You should see our wooden

    Stakes our

    Lapping flames

FOUNDING FATHER.

    Things seem older

    Overseas

    Like churches and bridges

    They'll always be older!

The Haiku Cherry Blossoms of Michigan

(*Blossoms*)

CHERRY BLOSSOM.
       Michigan water
              Tastes just like cherry wine
       All other states'

       Tastes like turpentine
              Sometimes I look like pillows
       I bloom once a year!

(*Blossoms falling*)

Kenneth Koch Designs the Set for *Hamlet* in Minnesota

KOCH.

        The knife buildings

        And the knife curtains

        The knife goblets

        And the knife lighting

        The knife levels

        And the knife bedchambers

        The knife swords

        And the knife poison

        Will set the knife stage

        For the knife father

        His knife ghost

        Walking the knife parapet

        Of the knife castle

        Looking out with our knife eyes

        At the knife night

        Rising like a moon knife

        Above the knifed audience

        Is my idea

        My overall

        Theme

Mississippi Goddamn

(A piano, water)

NINA SIMONE.
>Ne me quitte pas

MISSISSIPPI.
>You can't eat here

NINA SIMONE.
>Ne me quitte pas

MISSISSIPPI.
>You can't sit there

NINA SIMONE.
>Ne me quitte pas

MISSISSIPPI.
>I'm on fire! You're on fire!

NINA SIMONE.
>Mississippi goddam!

Missing You in Missouri

(A train station)

ME.
       I miss you

(A train passes by)

Academic Restrictions in Montana

(A schoolroom, a Student, a Teacher dressed as the Statue of Liberty)

STUDENT.

George Washington grew up in a log cabin and ate
pancakes with syrup and became president and spent a
lot of time taxing the timber industry

TEACHER.

Name the sightseers in the war of 1812

STUDENT.

Darwin!

TEACHER.

No! Where was Lincoln assassinated?

STUDENT.

In the Battle of Gettysburg

TEACHER.

And who killed him?

STUDENT.

The separation of church and state

TEACHER.

Now we are getting to the bottom of high finance and
standardized tests

STUDENT.

May I be excused?

TEACHER.

You are excused!

(Fireworks, flags)

The Boss Opens for Nebraska

BRUCE SPRINGSTEEN.
>I'm honored to open for you

NEBRASKA.
>Just you? No E Street Band?

BRUCE SPRINGSTEEN.
>Nope, just me

NEBRASKA.
>I liked the E Street Band

BRUCE SPRINGSTEEN.
>They're great, I agree

NEBRASKA.
>They really filled you out you know

BRUCE SPRINGSTEEN.
>Do you miss the saxophone?

(*Saxophone music*)

NEBRASKA.
>No hotter sax than the E Street Band

BRUCE SPRINGSTEEN.
>You know that's right!

(*More saxophone music*)

Kenneth Koch Plays Hamlet in Nevada

KOCH.
> I miss York…Yorek?…Yorick?

NEVADA.
> I miss Bugsy

(*Koch lifts up a skull, Nevada lifts up a skull*)

KOCH.
> I miss Denmark

NEVADA.
> I miss Vegas

(*Koch lifts up some tulips, Nevada lifts up a slot machine*)

KOCH.
> I miss Ophelia

NEVADA.
> I miss Marilyn

(*Koch lifts up a drowned woman, Nevada lifts up a blond wig*)

KOCH.
> Let's get married

NEVADA.
> I know just the place

(*Koch and Nevada proceed offstage with the wig and body toward the wedding*)

A Bus Stop in New Hampshire

BUS STOP.
>I want a train
>
>To come by and notice
>
>Me, a red sports
>
>Car going 90 mph
>
>Screeching to a stop
>
>Its rims spinning us
>
>Into infinity
>
>A plane, a jumbo jet
>
>To land
>
>A foot from the curb
>
>An air balloon, subway
>
>Submarine, rocket ship
>
>Streamliner, parachute
>
>Unicycle, a motorcycle
>
>With a mean
>
>Motherfucker revving
>
>The engine
>
>All night
>
>All night I'm ready!
>
>Everyone's so sick
>
>Of waiting, of

The nights of terror

The gnashing of teeth

New Jersey New Deco

(*The sound of coffee*)

WAITER.
    I love art

WAITRESS.
    You should

WAITER.
    I do

WAITRESS.
    This is the French Renaissance

WAITER.
    I thought it was Italian New Wave

WAITRESS.
    That's cinema

WAITER.
    Black-and-white movies and balloons

WAITRESS.
    Red balloons

WAITER.
    I thought black and white always meant a Renaissance

WAITRESS.
    This is New Jersey, you're thinking of Harlem

(*The sound of broken plates*)

New Mexico Calling Card

(*A Woman in a telephone booth*)

WOMAN.
>   Hola!

>   Holá?

>   Holá?!!

(*A Child enters dragging a bat and a piñata*)

CHILD.
>   La ventana de oportunidad está cerrada!

(*Phones ringing*)

New York New York Is a Hell of a Town

HOMELESS.

When I grew up I wanted to be a dentist and go surfing
on the weekends

HOMELESS.

I wanted to be a senator and rescue lost animals on
the weekends

HOMELESS.

My mother said no one with teeth like mine would ever
be a dentist

HOMELESS.

My father said that no one who killed his own fish
could be a senator

HOMELESS.

I brushed and listened to Dick Dale endlessly

HOMELESS.

I brought my tackle box to the steps of city hall

HOMELESS.

I never tanned, it was either whitest white or burn
burn burn

HOMELESS.

Those hooks had economic power!

HOMELESS.

I never learned to swim

HOMELESS.

I was jealous of other people's fly rods

(A Woman walks by in a swimsuit, leading a Small Fish)

HOMELESS AND HOMELESS.
    Surf's up!!!

King Kong in North Carolina

(A Prisoner in an electric chair)

PRISONER.

> I never touched her
>
> I never even saw her

(A Waiter enters)

> I would like
>
> Spaghetti and meatballs
>
> A strawberry shake
>
> Two cans of Coke
>
> Mashed potatoes and gravy
>
> One peach
>
> A glass of milk
>
> One apple
>
> A piece of chocolate cake

(The Waiter exits)

Speaking French in North Dakota

(*Rosy light on a rumpled bed, birds, cigarettes*)

MAN.
Merci

OTHER MAN.
Merci à vous

(*They disappear beneath the sheets*)

Oh Oh Oh Ohio

(*Fred Astaire and Ginger Rogers play tug-o'-war*)

FRED.

  Only in Ohio

GINGER.

  Could the rope get so tight

FRED.

  Only in Ohio

GINGER.

  Could you look so handsome!

FRED.

  Only in Ohio

GINGER.

  Could I look so beautiful!

FRED.

  Only in Ohio

GINGER.

  Could the covered bridges

FRED.

  Be so covered

GINGER.

  And the working poor

FRED.

  Run out to the movies

GINGER.

  Like a movie themselves!

FRED.

In tuxedos and Cinemascope!

(*Bubbles*)

Social Security and Welfare Reform Warm It Up at the Kitty-Kitty Club in Oklahoma City Oklahoma

SS.

One for the money

WR.

Two for the show

SS.

Three to get ready

WR.

Four to go

(They tap-dance slowly across the stage and back and then back again and off)

Sacagawea in Oregon

(A forest in Oregon, Sacagawea sits covered in a fever blanket)

SACAGAWEA.
> I'm on a coin!

(War drums)

The Haiku Poets of Pennsylvania

PENN.

I am a prison

My toothbrush is a sharp shank

The clouds are ex-cons

SYLVANIA.

I am a vampire

My mouth is a bloody bank

The moon is a tooth

Buddhist Invitations in Rhode Island

(*The music of smooth stones and lotus flowers*)

LAMA.

> Ahimsa is the beating heart of Buddhism and summarizes all virtue

COCKROACH.

> Where does it come from?

LAMA.

> It is rooted in the Vedas, in the figurines of living creatures

COCKROACH.

> So you would never crush me, even late at night while I dance along the edge of your bathtub?

LAMA.

> You mean crawling

COCKROACH.

> No I mean dancing

LAMA.

> Well, when you dance you look like you're crawling

COCKROACH.

> It's the dancing of the Noh theater
>
> You are the one
>
> Crawling!

BUSINESS REPLY MAIL

FIRST-CLASS MAIL   PERMIT NO. 43   PORT TOWNSEND WA

POSTAGE WILL BE PAID BY ADDRESSEE

Copper Canyon Press
PO Box 271
Port Townsend, WA 98368-9931

So, what do you think?

Book Title: _____

Comments: _____
_____
_____
_____

Can we quote you on that? ☐ yes ☐ no

Copper Canyon Press seeks to build the awareness of, appreciation of, and audience for a wide range of emerging and established American poets, as well as poetry in translation from many of the world's cultures, classical and contemporary. To receive our catalog, send us this postage-paid card or email your contact information to poetry@coppercanyonpress.org

NAME: _____

ADDRESS: _____

CITY: _____

STATE: _____ ZIP: _____

EMAIL: _____

☐ Send me *Editor's Choice*, a bimonthly email of poems from forthcoming titles.

COPPER CANYON PRESS

www.coppercanyonpress.org

What Do You Think of When You Think of South Carolina

SOUTH.
>Nothing really

CAROLINA.
>Beaches, water

SOUTH.
>Grains of sand and glass

CAROLINA.
>Glittering between

SOUTH.
>The toes

CAROLINA.
>Of a pretty girl

SOUTH.
>I made love to

CAROLINA.
>One night

SOUTH.
>Her swimsuit

CAROLINA.
>Like a second skin

SOUTH.
>Drowned beneath

CAROLINA.
>Her ankles

An Open Door in South Dakota

A CLOSED DOOR.

> There are moments
>
> On the outside
>
> And, as well, on the inside
>
> That could move
>
> A hard man
>
> To tears, finally
>
> Over the body
>
> Of his father, who
>
> Was also hard
>
> And who also
>
> Cried over the body
>
> Of his father
>
> On a night like this
>
> Looking out
>
> Over the road
>
> That brought him here
>
> And with him
>
> The point of sorrow
>
> The lucky
>
> Wooden nickel
>
> His father carried

In any number of pockets

(*The Door opens*)

The Tennessee Two-Step

(A large group of Tennesseans stomping out a two-step back and forth across the stage)

TENNESSEANS.
>This is the dance

(Pause)
>That won the war

(Pause)
>That put the bodies

(Pause)
>Of our sons

(Pause)
>And daughters

(Pause)
>Back together

(Pause)
>The dance

(Pause)
>That turned

(Pause)
>The sands into seas

(Pause)
>The night

(Pause)
>Into day

(Pause)

And night again

(*Jazz hands!*)

Kenneth Koch Plays Gertrude in Texas

(*Koch as Gertrude is tied to the back of a pickup truck*)

KOCH.

What are you doing?

HAMLET.

Scaring you

(*Very loud wind through the live oaks*)

Religious Rights in Utah

(*A Cattle Fence on the plains of Utah*)

THE COWS.

    I want to apologize

    For the fence

    Because the fence

    Won't apologize

    For itself

THE FENCE.

    I told you I would do it!

THE COWS.

    Then do it already!

THE FENCE.

    I'm sorry

    I was lost but now I'm found

Love Finds Time in Vermont

WOMAN.

> Can you believe it's been five years?

OTHER WOMAN.

> It's wonderful

WOMAN.

> You're wonderful

OTHER WOMAN.

> You're delightful

WOMAN.

> You're delicious

OTHER WOMAN.

> What time is it?

WOMAN.

> Midnight

Virginia Rebels

THE PEOPLE.

Revolution!

For the people!

For the economy!

For human rights!

Free unions!

Fair trade!

For the people!

THE REBELS.

I can't feel my arm!

Snow Falls Carefully in Washington

(*A field*)

ABE LINCOLN.
> I hated it there

GEORGE WASHINGTON.
> I felt I was happy

ABE LINCOLN.
> My hat is a tall smokestack

GEORGE WASHINGTON.
> My wig is a field covered in snow

(*Snow falls carefully*)

West Virginia Odyssey

(*The dark sea, a bedroom*)

O.

I could have sailed out there forever!

P.

I could have waited

Knitting and

Unknitting!

O.

You never slept with anyone else?

P.

No

O.

Because you never wanted to

P.

I wouldn't say that

O.

What would you say?

On the dark sea

On the wine-dark sea

Wisconsin Iliad

(*Troy*)

TROJAN HORSE.
> This pasture

ACHILLES.
> Was once a battlefield

HOMER.
> These hands

AGAMEMNON.
> Are made of line breaks
>
> And coed English department cocktail parties
>
> And salt
>
> And whey
>
> And curds!

Kenneth Koch Plays Laertes in Wyoming

(*Cowboy hats everywhere*)

KOCH.

      I had loved

      And felt

      Day and night

      That her legs

      Could fit

      Easily

      Over my shoulders

      And that

      As they say

      With a drop of the hat

      A wink of the eye

      Is that

      The kingdom

      Could be lifted

      Like a table, a chair

      And placed before me

      Where I could sit still

      A napkin floating

      Over my lap

      And eat my dinner

      And prepare myself

A Ghazal in Guam

(*a ghost walks out onto center stage*)

GHOST.

Is there anywhere I won't die? Maybe a place called Guam
where my body lives, drinking and singing about Guam

Last night I got so tired I don't think I even had a skeleton
beneath the sheets of my skin, it was like the fog in Guam

Last night every cell in my body became a little star, the tip
of a needle which punctured something that sounds like Guam

Last night everyone who has ever loved me was lifted up into
the sky where I could see the moon turning away from Guam

Last night there was no night, only the cold grass in the yard
being so quiet you thought it could have been the sky above Guam

I want to get up in the morning with all the teeth in my head, my
body whole, the twin trees in the yard happy to be living in Guam

(*the ghost disappears*)

The Minor League Sonnets of Puerto Rico

(*four batters approach the plate*)

BATTER 1:

>It's not the Screwball, the Knuckleball, or the Slider
>that spills my heart all over the diamond
>but the jet fighters
>imitating Ancient Mayans

BATTER 2:

>You're out!
>You're out!
>You're out!

BATTER 3:

>It's not the Splitter, the Slurve, or the Two-seam Fastball
>that has me rushing the pitcher
>but the palm trees calling
>my name: no hitter, no hitter

BATTER 4:

>You're still out!
>You're still out!
>You're still out!

About the Authors

Matthew Dickman lives in the state of Oregon.

Michael Dickman lives in the state of New Jersey.

Lannan Literary Selections

For two decades Lannan Foundation has supported the publication and distribution of exceptional literary works. Copper Canyon Press gratefully acknowledges their support.

LANNAN LITERARY SELECTIONS 2012

Matthew Dickman and Michael Dickman, *50 American Plays*

Michael McGriff, *Home Burial*

Tung Hui-Hu, *Greenhouses, Lighthouses*

James Arthur, *Charms Against Lightning*

Natalie Diaz, *When My Brother Was an Aztec*

RECENT LANNAN LITERARY SELECTIONS FROM COPPER CANYON PRESS

Michael Dickman, *Flies*

Laura Kasischke, *Space, In Chains*

Deborah Landau, *The Last Usable Hour*

Sarah Lindsay, *Twigs and Knucklebones*

Heather McHugh, *Upgraded to Serious*

W.S. Merwin, *Migration: New & Selected Poems*

Valzhyna Mort, *Collected Body*

Taha Muhammad Ali, *So What: New & Selected Poems, 1971-2005,* translated by Peter Cole, Yahya Hijazi, and Gabriel Levin

Lucia Perillo, *Inseminating the Elephant*

Ruth Stone, *In the Next Galaxy*

John Taggart, *Is Music: Selected Poems*

Jean Valentine, *Break the Glass*

C.D. Wright, *One Big Self: An Investigation*

Dean Young, *Fall Higher*

For a complete list of Lannan Literary Selections from Copper Canyon Press, please visit Partners on our Web site:
www.coppercanyonpress.org

Since 1972, Copper Canyon Press has fostered the work of emerging, established, and world-renowned poets for an expanding audience. The Press thrives with the generous patronage of readers, writers, booksellers, librarians, teachers, students, and funders—everyone who shares the belief that poetry is vital to language and living.

MAJOR SUPPORT HAS BEEN PROVIDED BY:

The Paul G. Allen Family Foundation

Amazon.com

Anonymous

Arcadia Fund

John Branch

Diana and Jay Broze

Beroz Ferrell & The Point, LLC

Mimi Gardner Gates

Golden Lasso, LLC

Gull Industries, Inc.
on behalf of William and Ruth True

Carolyn and Robert Hedin

Lannan Foundation

Rhoady and Jeanne Marie Lee

National Endowment for the Arts

New Mexico Community Foundation

Penny and Jerry Peabody

Joseph C. Roberts

Cynthia Lovelace Sears and Frank Buxton

Washington State Arts Commission

Charles and Barbara Wright

To learn more about underwriting Copper Canyon Press titles,
please call 360-385-4925 ext. 103

The Chinese character for poetry is made up of two parts: "word" and "temple." It also serves as pressmark for Copper Canyon Press.

The poems are set in Caslon.
Book design and composition by Phil Kovacevich.
Printed on archival-quality paper at McNaughton & Gunn, Inc.